A Different Type of Church Girl

TREVI BOOKER PERSHAY

Possibilitea Publishing, a division of Ark of Safetea
Possibiliteapublishing@gmail.com

Contact the author at: trevipershay@aol.com
ISBN 10:1720701148
ISBN-13:978-1720701149

DEDICATION

This book is dedicated to my heart Pearl Booker-Carter.

CONTENTS

ACKNOWLEDGMENTS

ROMANS 13: 7 – "Render therefore to all their dues: tribute to whom tribute is due, custom to whom custom, fear to whom fear, honor to whom honor."

My Family

Eddie Oliphant – My Dad! I met him a few times in life and his smile was contagious. RIP!

Margaret Sheppard – My Mom! Thanks for being you and teaching me to be tough and strong during my journey of life. Also shout out to my stepdad Leroy McIntyre

Roy Pershay, my husband, we've been through a lot and thanks for coming to every play I produced and words of strength when I needed it. Rodnisha & Arielle Pershay, my daughters, who have stood by my side when others have walked away.

Cassie Moore, Towanda Booker-Fair and Sharkey Sheppard – my loving sisters

Gwendolyn Booker, Trina Booker-Lightner, Aunt Frances Booker, Darcel Booker, Janique Egerton, Tammy Devine Aunt Eleanor McCray (the one who taught me how to pray) and Aunt Ella McIntyre for supporting my plays and encouraging me. Big shout-out to my PDM Students and parents, I love you all.

The Wise Counsel of Friends

Bishop-Elect Dr. Courtney Bradley – thank you for 20 years of friendship and being my spiritual leader and mentor. God used you to pour into my brokenness and taught me the word of God like never before. You've always encouraged me and embraced my personal ministry.

Bishop Rufus Mahon – you have proven yourself to be a good friend and mentor. You tell me the truth whether I receive it or not. You stood by my side when I slipped, and helped me get back up. Thank you to your wife, Alison Mahon, your prayers have encouraged me through my tough journey.

Tinika Thomas, my business partner and my best friend, thank you

for reading this book and pushing me every day. Andre Foreman –
always having my back and being there and a true friend. Dwayne
Loadholt – thank you believing in me and pushing me. Thank you
for the opportunity in hearing God to ordain me as Elder and
Youth Pastor of Living Water Church, that helped me get to where
I am today. A special thank you to Shantana Rogers, Arielle
Pershay and Na-Quasia Rogers for being the first to read this book
15 years ago when it was in draft form.
Best friends from school – Kim French and Felicia Thomas for
being my cheerleaders and investors in my projects.

Thank you to everyone who supported my plays:
Christian Scrooge, Love Don't Live Here Anymore, Tales of 2
Spirts – Power vs Position, Drama High, Fifteen and Grown I and
II, The Journey of a Blackman, The Journey of a Black Woman,
Real Men Do Cry, Black Women Are We Crazy or Nah?, The
Curse Between My Legs, Christmas in the Hood The Defiled Bed
– Pain between the sheets and Thou Shall Not Kill – When Murder
Becomes the New Black and in production (2018) Not My Child,
Blinded by Love – See No Evil, Hear No Evil and Keep the Evil
and (2019) The Defiled Bed 2 – the Awakening and The Secrets
Within.

Thank you all from the bottom of my heart!!!!

AUTHOR'S NOTES
The Writer's Corner

January 31, 2018, I was admitted in the hospital for what I thought was a general cold or something. I thought to myself, this is something that I could shake off in a day or two. Besides I'm thinking to myself I've survived 3 strokes, 2 car accidents and a mild heart attack. I'm sure I will beat this thing, whatever it is. As the evening fell, I found myself not able to breathe and the cough was hurting so bad that it prohibited me from speaking.

I was diagnosed with a very rare case of pneumonia. It was so rare that the doctors couldn't put a name on it. It caused me to remain in the hospital for 3 weeks and rehabilitation for 6 days. This was by far the hardest trial I have ever experienced. I was the youngest person on the ward and the sickest. Many of the other patients were 75 and older. I was in ICU for seven days, and the rest of my stay I was in the respiratory unit.

I forgot to mention that I was laid off from my job on January 9th, my last day was January 31st. After I dropped off my company inventory, I took ill. However, I was confident that I would get another job, I wasn't too worried about that. My goal was to focus on the grants' deadline for my organization, writing my book, as well as upcoming plays. I though thought to myself, I will use the time off wisely. However, being sick, I lost out on job opportunities, $20,000 for grants and had financial issues.

Let me be transparent for a moment, I was angry at God. I wanted to know why the hell did he choose me? I'm like, "Hey God, I know a hell of a lot of people you can test. I had a plan, a strategy and a vision, and it all came tumbling down in a few hours." Let's just say that being in the hospital, I picked up my Bible and it opened to the book of Job. Oh no, I thought to myself, who wants a trial like this man? I refused to read it. As the days went by, I began to get sicker and weaker. Again, I picked up the Bible and it would always open to the book of Job.

I have a new outlook for Job and what the Lord put him through. When I tell you, I studied the book of Job. I knew my trusting in God was on another level that I had never seen before. I had no unemployment insurance, no health insurance, and I was stuck in a nursing home. The nursing home had a plan to keep me there for a whole month. I was like I don't think so. Every night I would walk with the oxygen machine that I was attached to and kept singing praises unto God. I was determined to walk again. The nursing home staff left me to myself for 6 days without attending to me. They would only medicate me and move on. I had to fight even inside that place. I was able to speak for myself unlike the other patients that were there. However, when they came to rehabilitate me, I was already walking, standing and learning how to breathe without the oxygen tank. They were so surprised and kept checking my ID bracelet to see if I was the right person. With prayer and determination, I signed myself out of there.

When I tell you learning how to walk and breathe on my own was so difficult. Everyone kept saying God is going to do a quick work. Guess what? It didn't happen like that for me. I cried because all I wanted to do was dance, work, breathe, run, work out and be active in my church again. Watch this, I didn't take it lying down. I fought against what the doctors said I will never do again. As time went on during my healing process, I kept getting bad news from the doctors. Seems like ever since this pneumonia entered my body it brought so much other craziness with it. I was diagnosed with Glaucoma, partial blood clot in the back of my brain, vertigo and a slightly damaged left lung. Now while all this is taking place in my life, I keep walking, shouting, dancing, running upstairs and being active. I figured my lungs would have to catch up with the spirit of healing. Then I started looking for employment. Meanwhile, the doctors told me that I would not be able to work for a year, and it would be wise to get some type of social security disability insurance. I wasn't trying to hear them.

Listen, while I was in the hospital, I was ministering to those that needed it. When I was in the nursing home, I encouraged the staff through the word of God. My assignment was not over, and God didn't tell me to stop working, so I started looking for employment. Walking to my interviews with a pump in my hand to help with the breathing. I was determined to get my life back. I had too much to do than to be depressed by what the doctors said, when I believe what God said. This was my trial and I had to pass it. Like Job, I was losing my grants, health, my ability to write and

I lost students in my organization. Even in Job's distress of how God could allow something so evil to come against him because of his faithfulness towards God. I felt the same way. In Job 7:21, Job cried out to God and said "Why do you not pardon my offenses and forgive my sins? For I will soon lie down in the dust you will search for me and I will be no more." In other words, I feel like I'm going to die in this thing. That is how I felt. I'm like what the heck just happened to me. Job passed his test and receive more from God. Just like me.

Trevi

A PRAYING GRANDMOTHER

I could hear my name being called in my slumber. "Zoya, Chile get out of that bed and prepare for church. Zoya! I'm not going to call you anymore!" The voice of my baritone grandmother coming from the kitchen. "Zoya get up now!" With a big sigh, I threw the covers over my head and yelled from underneath them, "Nana, please just five more minutes?" "Zoya, get up," Nana yells! "You know how your grandfather feels about tardiness in getting to the Lord's house. After all, he is the Pastor." Nana looked toward my room door and yelled, "Zoya, get up!" I yelled back, "Ok Nana, I'm getting up!"

I threw the warm covers off me and stretched my long legs and arms from out of my bed. As I inhaled, I could smell the breakfast coming from the kitchen. I ran into the kitchen to see what else Nana was preparing. I could see the grits in a large pot, squeezed orange juice, turkey sausages, eggs, butter biscuits and bacon just calling me to the table. Nana knew how to work the kitchen, and she was cooking Sunday dinner too. The baked ham, peas and rice, apple pie, collard greens, peas and my favorite macaroni and cheese. I was hypnotized by the food that was prepared before me. The Bible does say in Psalm 23:5 "He prepares a table before me in the presence of my enemies..." At that very moment, the enemy was my growling stomach, and I was ready to eat. Thank you, Lord, for the table and I sat down to eat. My stomach was fighting with my back about who would eat first. I felt this slap on the back of my head, and it came from Nana. I turned to her in frustration and Nana started to fuss. "Zoya, I know you're not sitting at this table not washed and dressed. Zoya, uncleanliness is the sign of the devil so go in the bathroom and wash up." "Yes Nana," I answered with my eyes cast down. One thing about Nana when she gives you that look is it cuts into your gut.

Defeated, I went to my room, made up my bed and sized up the clothes that Nana picked out for me to wear to church. I wished Nana would just let me pick out my own clothes. She really had no taste. All my dresses looked like they were birthed from a sack of potatoes. Nana didn't believe in colors. She made me wear browns, beige or black to church. I felt like I was mourning or

4

something. Then I remembered a dress my momma brought for me when she lived here. It was pink and yellow, my two favorite colors. I, turned to the closet and started to dig for the dress. "I know I hid that dress in the back of the closet. Oh my God, here it is!" She said in excitement holding up the dress, and ran to her full-length mirror and examined the dress, pressed up against her pajamas. "Wow! This is such a pretty color and it looks like I grew a bit because the dress appears to be shorter." I could smell her mother's perfume mixed with cigarettes on her dress. The memories of that day were so painful. Nana walked into my room and I looked to find that furious look on her face. "Zoya, throw that dress in the garbage." She spoke through gritted teeth. With tears welling up in my eyes, I said, "Nana this is all that I have left of mommy, and I'm not going to throw it away." Nana's eyes bulged out of her head like I had never seen before. Nana came over to me and tried to snatch the dress out of my hands, but I held on to it for dear life. "Let it go Zoya." "Nana, please stop. This was a gift from my mother. It's all I have of her." Nana slapped my face so hard that I felt like an ice skater performing a 360 spin. I hit the floor with the dress still in my hands. Grandpa Joe ran into my room and separated Nana from me.

"Mary! What is all this foolery about? Huh?" Nana turned to grandpa, pointed at my dress and said, "It's about that ridiculous dress that her mother gave her." Grandpa looked at Nana and then back at me. He said, "Mary, our daughter Zina, gave Zoya that dress, and she has a right to have it. You can't just erase her momma's memory Mary. It's all she has left." As Grandpa made his plea to Nana, I felt it was safe to get up off the floor and wipe the tears from my eyes. Grandpa turned to me and said, "Go shower, get dressed and then eat your breakfast Zo." Then Grandpa turned to Nana and said, "It's time to prepare for church and I'm not letting no demon ruin my Sunday morning. As the Pastor of Greater Love & Hope Baptist Church and the head of this house, I speak peace!" Nana gave grandpa one of her deadly stares and walked away. Grandpa and I both looked at each other when Nana left the room. While holding the dress in my hands, I could feel Grandpa, and I knew what he was thinking. I took the dress and threw it in the closet to make peace. Grandpa walked over to me and he gave me such a big hug and said, "Thank you." I smiled and said, "Grandpa we won't let this dress be the demon of our day." Grandpa smiled and walked out of my room. I was sitting on my bed pissed-off, because once again Nana won the fight.

After taking a long shower and speaking to the Lord, I felt better. I walked into my room and pulled out that ugly black dress that Nana originally put out for me to wear to church. All I kept hearing was the scripture Grandpa taught me, Ephesians 6:2, "Honor thy mother and father." Although my flesh was talking back to me very loudly. My flesh said, "Technically she is not your mother, so you don't have to honor her." I said to my flesh, "Be quiet. Nana is all the mother I have right now, so she is fulling the assignment until my momma comes back." Sighing, I put on that ugly black dress, and I tied my long curly hair into a ponytail. Once I was dressed, I entered the kitchen to find Grandpa, Nana and nosey Mother Mills at the table. Mother Mills was Nana's best friend, as well as the motivator behind Nana's bad behavior. I prayed to the Lord to give me strength, and I walked to the table and took a seat. Nana was still angry because she kept talking to Mother Mills while ignoring Grandpa and me. When I would ask Nana to past the butter she would ignore my request. Grandpa passed it to me and winked at me, which made me smile. Grandpa focused on his sermon and I ate in silence. The doorbell rang, and my cousins, aunts and uncles entered the house and the noise was welcoming to me. I felt my spirit being lifted and I was happy to be distracted from Nana's meanness. We were all ready to go to church together and it looked like the Lord answered my prayer by bringing peace in our house. Off to church we went.

Service was amazing, and Grandpa preached a good sermon. I enjoyed how Grandpa would break down the Word of God so that everyone could obtain a great understanding of what God wanted us to hear. Grandpa preached about having compassion like Jesus. Luke 23:34 says, "Father forgive them for they know not what they do." What's amazing is when Jesus was on the cross he was being crossed. Grandpa said, "Jesus was still pleading to God on our behalf even while he was being mistreated." It was good medicine for our souls and everyone loved the message except for Nana. Jesus' seven last words on the cross were not about who wronged him or defending himself. Nana would sit in the pews with a mean spirit. She would only stand up when Pastor would say, "God is watching how we treat others." Nana stood up waving her hands, and looking at me as if that was meant for me. Then Nana sat with her arms folded because Grandpa rebuked her by telling her to stay in the flow of the message. Nevertheless, the best part of the service is when new souls came to the altar and gave their lives to Jesus. I'd get so emotional with that part of the service. I've watched people come to the altar with such a heavy burden, tears in their eyes and hope in their hearts. People just wanted a change in their lives and Grandpa was so awesome when he prayed and hugged people. Grandpa always let me assist him by welcoming the new converts in love and a hug.

After service, everyone was cleaning the church and Mother Mills came over to Grandpa and told him that Nana was in the car because she wasn't feeling her best. Then Mother Mills walked over to me and said, "Zoya, don't let the devil use you to hurt your Nana. She's all you got, and God will strike you down," she pointed her finger in my face, "If you don't treat the elders right." It says so in the Bible. Enjoy your afternoon." Mother Mills walked away from me. I stood in silence because I didn't want to be disrespectful to Mother Mills. Grandpa came over and took the broom out of my hand, and asked Deacon Morris to finish cleaning up the church because he had to take Nana home. Grandpa held my hand as we walked to the car. Lo and behold Nana was sitting in the front seat looking straight ahead as if she didn't want to look at me. At this point, I was in no mood for Nana because I was going to hold the Word of God close to my heart. The word was forgive them that hurt you.

We finally got home, the house was filled with the scent of Nana's food. I went in my room to wash up, change my clothes and finish up my essay that was due tomorrow. Nana called Grandpa and me to the dinner table once she heated up the food. When Grandpa and I entered the kitchen, Nana took her food and went into her bedroom and closed the door behind her. Grandpa looked exhausted, but he kept the conversation going without Nana. "Zo, did you enjoy the sermon today?" My eyes lit up and I smiled, "Yes." We were laughing at the funny things that happened in service. Grandpa loved when I made fun of Deacon Jones shouting. I loved to hear the richness of Grandpas' laughter.

Grandpa was so handsome. He was 6 feet tall, had green eyes, beautiful olive skin, white teeth, short beard and beautiful waves in his hair. I could tell that he was drop dead gorgeous when he was younger. Grandpa and I started singing some church songs while cleaning up the kitchen. Next thing you know, we heard a banging sound and it got our attention.

Nana opened the bedroom door with such force that it knocked down the picture hanging on the wall. Grandpa and I looked at Nana, and she was angry. Grandpa immediately rushed over to make sure Nana was ok. Grandpa took Nana's plate from her hand and examined her. Then he kissed Nana on the forehead and told her to rest. Nana of course liked the attention going towards her and she played into Grandpa's affection for her. Grandpa picked Nana up and took her into the bedroom to undress her and lay her down. I was sitting in the chair thinking to myself that Nana was jealous of my relationship with my Grandpa. How weird was that? I shrugged my shoulders and I continued to clean up the kitchen. Grandpa entered the kitchen and touched my shoulder and said, "Your grandmother needs you." In my mind, I thought that the only thing Nana needed was a slap in the face. I turned to Grandpa with a smile on my face and said, "Sure Grandpa."

I walked into Nana's room and braced myself for what I was about to see. To my surprise, Nana had this hateful look on her face and she said to me, "I threw out that dress, so you'll never see it again." I was furious, and I stood up to face Nana with a boldness that I had never experienced before. I stepped close to her and said, "Why would you throw something away that means so much to me? You will never erase my mother's memory no matter how hard you try." Nana sat up in the bed, the icepack on her head fell to the floor. Now she was even more angry. "Listen to me little girl, you will do what I say while living under this roof." She poked me in my chest. Nana was still putting her hands on me. I had to maintain my composure and I said, "I have no choice, but to respect your decision and rules in your house as you say. But let me make this clear Nana, my mother will always be in my heart and you can't take that away from me no matter how you treat me."

Then before I knew it, something sharp came down on my head, and I passed out. When I woke up I had a very bad headache and something dry and sticky was on my hair. I couldn't really turn my head because it hurt so bad, and then a man in a white coat was standing over me checking my head. I asked where I was. The doctor's name was Dr. David Grinn and he said, "Well hello sleeping beauty. Glad to see you're up. How are you feeling? Can you tell me what happened to you?" Next thing I know Nana was by my bedside holding my hand with tears in her eyes. Nana looked at me while gripping my hand and said, "I told the doctor we were playing, and you hit your head on the edge of the dresser in my room." Nana looked scared and it all came back to me. I remembered the fight Nana and I were having. After I told her that she would never erase my mother's memory. Nana pushed me, I pushed her back, and I turned to leave her room. Nana called me a whore and then hit me over the head with something. Dr. Grinn distracted my thoughts and said, "That was a nasty fall young lady." I removed Nana's hand from mine and asked for Grandpa. "Where is my Grandpa?" Dr. Grinn saw that I was getting upset with Nana in the room and asked her to leave and get her husband. Nana insisted that she stay in the room, but I refused to let Nana win this fight. I thought to myself that this woman just tried to kill me.

Grandpa entered the room and Nana left apparently upset. Then Dr. Grinn left us alone to review my CAT scan. Grandpa held my hand and kissed it. Grandpa whispered in my ear, "As you get older, you're becoming a lot like your mother and well…. your grandmother gets upset about it. Be patient with her Zo." I looked at Grandpa and said, "I won't tell the doctors what really happened because I know that they will lock Nana up." Dr. Grinn, came in and told us I had to stay overnight for more tests. I was given something for pain and I remember Grandpa kissing me on the forehead. My eyes were heavy from the medicine and I began to get sleepy, and I could see Nana staring at me with no emotion. I couldn't keep my eyes open and then I started to remember. I remembered the stories now, and I fell into a deep sleep.

GRANDPA JOE

Joseph and Mary Walsh were married the Fourth of July, Summer of 1972. It was one of the hottest days of the year in Macon, Georgia. Joseph was the most sort after bachelor in Macon. Every woman wanted him, tried to get him and worked with him to have him in their bed. Joseph was a respectful man and treated women the way he wanted his mother to be treated. Mr. Gary Wilson invited Joseph to his home to discuss a civil rights' issue he was having. While Joseph was visiting the home he caught the eye of Mr. Wilson's only daughter Mary. Mary reminded Joseph of his mother, frail, beautiful and simple. Mary wasn't flashy like many of the women Joseph had known. Mary was an outsider of Georgia, she grew up in Albany, New York. However, Joseph was so attracted to Mary that he fell in love with her at first sight. As Joseph started to date Mary, and showed up to church with her, many women were jealous. The church membership increased just because people wanted to take a good look at the drably Mary Wilson.

Joseph's law firmed worked closely with the NAACP in civil rights' issues for black people. After 10 years of working in his law firm, Joseph decided to answer the call to God and the church. Joseph decided to leave his practice in the capable hands of his brother Ray and staff. Joseph was now the Pastor of Friendship Baptist Church of Christ. Joseph held a master's degree in law and a master's degree in Religious Studies. Joseph stood 6 feet tall, 280 lbs., and was a very attractive man. Today was an important day because Joseph was marrying the woman that God had chosen for him. With all the excitement around today, Joseph thought about his mother. Joseph walked over to his desk and picked up the picture of his mother, rubbed his fingers across her picture. As Joseph looked down at his mother's photo on his desk those childhood memories came back. Although, Barbara Ann, was not living, she was the reason why he became a successful lawyer.

When Joseph was a child he would often ask his mother who his father was. Joseph's friends would always make fun of his hair texture and the color of his skin. Joseph was neither light skinned nor dark skinned. Joseph was somewhere in the middle, and his green eyes made him stand out for sure. Barbara Ann sat Joseph down when he was 10 years old, and said, "Son I need to tell you why you ain't got no daddy." Barbara Ann was not educated, but she was loving to her son. "Come in here and take a seat because I'm only gonna tell it once. I believe you only need one time to tell a bad story. You hear me boy?" Joseph looked into his mothers' light brown eyes and smiled, "Yes mama."

"Joseph, when I was a little girl my momma got real sick one day, and she sent me to work in her place. My momma was all business and she was the only one keeping money in the house. My step-dad was no good, he was out drinking all the time and sleeping with other women. So, my momma had to oversee the home. Momma gave me instructions on what I needed to do for the following day. Next morning, I had to get up at 4am so that I could be at the Lints' house at 6am. Momma said, "Barbara Ann, all you have to do is scrub the floors, take this dinner, it's already made. All they have to do is heat it up. Also wash Mrs. Lint's clothes, take out the garbage and wait for her outside on the back porch for the money. Make sure you get home before it gets dark you hear me girl?' I answered momma, 'Yes Ma, do the chores and get home before it gets dark'."

"So, I arrived that morning at the Lints' home on time like momma said at 6am, and I did what I was supposed to do. Mrs. Lint had a headache and she gave me momma's pay and told me to go home. I thanked Mrs. Lint, closed the door behind me and headed downstairs so I could go home. Mr. Lint walked into the kitchen, blocked my exit to leave the house. I stood back puzzled. I tried to go around him, and he blocked me from leaving the kitchen. I said, 'Mr. Lint, your wife said that I'm done for the day and I can go home. Momma cooked dinner and it's on the counter waiting for you to eat it.' Mr. Lint kept asking me questions and staring at me real funny. As a matter a fact, he was watching me in everything I was doing that day. Momma made me cover myself to not show any curves. She said it would keep my innocence for a while. Old Mr. Lint asked me to take my scarf off my head so that he could see my nigger hair. I replied, 'No sir Mr. Lint. My momma is waiting for me to come and I tried to run past him.' Mr. Lint pushed me really hard and I fell on the kitchen floor. Mr. Lint bent down and snatched the scarf from my head. My long, black, thick hair fell flowing down my back. Mr. Lint said, 'You look better than all those other niggers in your town. I guess you're half Indian or something,' with that scary laugh he had. Mr. Lint went and poured himself a drink and offered me one and I said, 'No thank you sir, I reckon you let me leave.' He demanded that I drink the dark liquid in the pretty crystal glass. I shook my head in fear because I didn't want to drink it."

"Mr. Lint grabbed me by my hair from the floor, and I opened my mouth to scream. Then he picked up the bottle that had the brown liquor in it and poured it in my mouth. I started to choke, and he laughed at me. I finally got myself together, but the brown liquor had me feeling dizzy. Mr. Lint was standing there staring at me asking my age, and I told him I was thirteen. I said, 'I have to leave now,' and I headed toward the door and made it outside. I couldn't walk once I was outside. I was hot and dizzy at the same time. I fell on the grass outside the house, and suddenly I was being pulled by my hair. I was kicking and screaming hoping that someone would hear me. I was dragged into the barn and thrown on top of the hay. Mr. Lint ripped off my undergarments and he raped me. I don't remember what happened because I passed out. All I could remember was the smell of that demon liquor and the pain between my legs. The pain was so unbearable that I passed out. The next day Mr. Urick who worked for the Lints, found me bleeding and laying in the barn. Mr. Urick and his wife bathed me and carried me home to momma. Once my momma saw me, she already knew what took place, and she held me in her arms and rocked me. I stopped going to school because I was pregnant with Mr. Lint's child. I was mad because I had to have a baby that I didn't want."

Joseph looked down with tears falling from his eyes listening to his mother's painful story. Now he understood why he looked different. It was because his father was a white man and a rapist. Barbara Ann could see how this was affecting her son, and she touched him lightly on his arm. "Joseph, the way you ended up in my belly was wrong, but when you came out, it was right." "Momma, why no one helped you?" Joseph respond angrily. "Black folks had no voice, therefore, had no power Joe. Not you Joseph Clay Walsh! No sir! You gonna be my lawyer, Son. I'm working real hard to put you through one of those fancy schools.

Joe, one day you're going to make me proud and make Mr. Lint pay for what he did to me. When you get your degree, we will go after his property, being that you're his kin. You have a right and so do I. Now give me a big hug and she laughed. You're momma's big man."

The loud knock on the door interrupted Joseph's thoughts. Raymond opened the door and entered the room. "Hey, big brother are you ready for… You alright Joe?" Joseph smiled at his brother, "I'm good best man, how are you?" "Why so quiet Bro? Getting cold feet?" Raymond started to punch his older brotherly playfully. Joseph blocked his brother's hits and threw a towel at him. They both laughed. "What's going on Joe?" Raymond asked. "I was thinking about momma and how I wished she was here to see me get married." Raymond hugged his brother and said, "Mom would have been real proud Joe. You already know how proud you made her when you went after Mr. Lint and rightfully asked for your inheritance at the will reading."

Raymond took the article that was framed on the wall and read from it: "Joseph Clay Walsh DNA proves that he is the rightful heir to the Lints' wealth. The brutal rape of Barbara Ann Walsh at 13 years old sent the community in such a rage that all Lint's enterprises were boycotted, which pressured the Lints to turn over shares of stock to Joseph Clay Walsh." Raymond laughed, "Who would ever think that Mrs. Lint was more on our side than her husband? The day she came to momma in that courthouse and said that she believed her husband raped her and that you looked just like Mr. Lint. Now that made momma proud," and Raymond hung the frame back on the wall. Joseph smiled, "I remember that day and how Mrs. Lint wanted to be in my life thereafter and good to momma. Poor Mr. Lint had too much of that brown liquor which caused him to hang himself. See Raymond, God has a way of working things out." "Listen big brother momma is in heaven looking down on you, and I'm sure she's proud of you. She would be even happier knowing that you are about to become a Pastor and Overseer of your own church. Momma was always reading the Bible and teaching us the Word of God. The only problem was that you were listening to the Word of God more than I was." Joseph smiled and said, "Well like momma said, 'a good man's steps are ordered by the Lord'," they both quoted it at the same time and laughed.

"Joe, listen if you have any doubts about this marriage this is the time to bail out now brother." Joseph smiled, "I'm good and I found what I'm looking for in a good wife." "Joe," Ray turned around to face him while fixing his bow tie on his tuxedo, "why Mary? Let's keep it real she looks more like Mary with the little lamb, and Marcy was the little Red Riding hood. Everyone thought you would marry Marcy. I'm not judging your taste Joe so don't look at me like that. I'm just asking why Mary?" Joseph looked at his brother in the eye and replied, "I love her Ray," and turned back to the mirror to continue fixing his bow tie. "Don't worry little brother I know what I'm doing. The Bible says, 'when a man finds a wife he finds a good thing,' Proverbs 18:22." The music started, and Ray and Joe knew that was the cue to enter the church. Both Ray and Joe headed toward the door and looked at each other for a moment not saying a word. Ray hugged his brother and said, "I'm happy for you Joe, now let's get you married and watch Red Riding Hood turn green."

HOMECOMING SURPRISE

"I can't open my eyes! Oh my God what is happening to me? Why is it so dark in this room?" I had to try and open my eyes. It felt like glue was holding them together. Finally, I fought to open my eyes and I could see the room now, but it was so blurry. I blinked a few times to allow my vision to come into focus. I was looking around and I saw all these tubes in my arms and in my nose. Then my eyes travelled to the edge of my bed, and I saw Grandpa Joe praying with his head buried in his arms. It looked as if he had been crying, and he looked very sad. I was trying to open my mouth to call his name, but my mouth was so dry. I could feel the tube in my throat that prevented me from calling for help or speaking. I closed my eyes not understanding what was taking place, and hot tears roll down my cheeks. I prayed inwardly, "Lord what is going on here? Let someone help me before I panic." The nurse who came into my room must have heard my prayers, and she walked over to me with excitement and yelled, "The patient is awake!"

Grandpa Joe jumped up and stood over me with tears falling from his eyes and kissed my forehead. "Zoya, you're a miracle baby. The Lord heard my prayers." Dr. Grinn walked in and said, "Hey Zoya welcome back to the living." What was he talking about? I was just sleeping for a few hours. Did I look that bad? Then the nurse pulled the tube out of my throat and I choked really hard. My throat felt like it was on fire. Dr. Grinn gave Grandpa Joe a sippy cup with cool water for me to drink. "Yes!" I thought to myself, "Finally this desert can leave my mouth so that I can talk." I welcomed the cool taste of water in my mouth. As I was sipping the water, my vision was in tact, I realized someone was missing from the picture. It was Nana. Suddenly my body let me know that I had been lying in bed for quite some time. I could feel the bed sores that developed on my buttocks, and my body was hurting all over. I opened my mouth and the only sound I could produce was a whisper. "What happened to me," I asked Dr. Grinn? Dr. Grinn informed me that I was in a coma for two months. Apparently, when I hit my head it caused a blood clot to my brain. I was thinking to myself, "Two months?? Oh my God the homework that I will have to do when I get out of here." I really just wanted to go home, and go back to school to see my friends.

Dr. Grinn was really a very nice, kind and handsome man. I think I had a crush on Dr. Grinn. However, I knew that he was too old, and I wasn't really sure what to do with a boy, let alone a man. Nana walked in my room as Dr. Grinn was talking to me. Dr. Grinn really made me smile a lot. Nana said in her stern voice, "Dr. Grinn, I'm sure you have other patients to see, please don't let my granddaughter hold you up." Dr. Grinn, looked over at Nana and said, "Not every doctor can say they have a miracle patient on their hands. Beside this patient gets special attention and I don't mind at all." Nana stared at him so hard that it made me uncomfortable. Dr. Grinn, noticed the change in my attitude and looked at Nana. "Mrs. Walsh, please make sure that my patient stays in good spirits. That is all part of her recovery." Before he walked out he whispered something to Nana, and I could tell that whatever Dr. Grinn said to her, made her upset.

Nana walked over to my bed and said, "I'm glad you're ok Zoya. Next time you need to be more careful about how you fall." I looked at her for a long time not saying anything. I remembered she hit me which caused my fall. However, I wouldn't go there because in my heart I had already forgiven her. Flesh was like, "Oh no, lock her up honey! You are way too kind. Go and fill out a police report and lock Nana up." I had to shake my head at my inner thoughts and remembered what Grandpa Joe taught us in Bible class. Grandpa Joe said that it's not our job to seek revenge on those that have done us wrong. Deuteronomy 32:35, "Vengeance is mine, their foot shall slip in due time." Therefore, I will keep my peace and let the Lord fight this battle. Nana started small talk with me and I just sat there listening to her ramble on about nothing. I guess this was Nana's way of saying that she was sorry that she was the reason why I was there. I just kept my eyes cast down looking towards the door hoping that Grandpa Joe or someone would come through the door and save me from this lady. Suddenly, my room door burst open and I heard someone say, "Zo!" I looked up and there she was. It was my momma. I got so excited that I threw the sheets off me and pushed past Nana to get to my mother. I moved too fast and got dizzy. Nana caught me and said, "Slow down Zoya." Momma rushed to my aid and grabbed me in her arms. That familiar smell of cigarettes and perfume was a welcoming treat to me. Momma and I didn't let each other go for a while, and I couldn't stop crying. I knew God heard my prayers and he answered them. "Thank you, God. Thank you for your power to bring me back to life and bringing my momma home. God I'm so grateful." As I started to thank God out loud it made momma thank him as well. God was truly in the midst of our union.

Two weeks later I was released from the hospital and finally back at home. Life at Nana's house was certainly different now that momma was staying with us. Grandpa Joe was more excited than I was that momma was home. Momma would walk me to school and when I came home she was there to help me with my homework. Grandpa Joe wanted to write a book, and momma encouraged him to share his sermons with the world. Everyone was happy, except Nana. Nana pretended to be happy, but she really wasn't. Momma stayed her distance from Nana by not getting in her way and only helped when needed.

Today was a half day at school and I couldn't wait to get home to see momma. As I entered the foyer of the house, I hung up my rain coat and took off my boots. I was lost in my thoughts on how to ask momma about boys. I really liked this boy in my class, and I didn't know much about boys. How could I be 14 years old, and not know anything about boys? I wanted to know about boys and I needed to know because they were all around me. When I asked Nana, she would say boys were made from the devil. Nana would say the devil made boys to ruin us girls. I said, "Well wasn't Grandpa Joe a boy before he was a man?" She said, "It was a different time," and then dismissed me. I could never figure out that story or Nana. As I was walking up the stairs, I could hear Nana and Momma arguing, almost screaming at each other. I ran into the kitchen to see what was going on. Nana was saying awful things to momma. "Zina, I want you out of my house and out of our lives." "Mother, that's fine by me, but understand this, I'm taking Zoya with me." "You will not take Zoya anywhere you gave up your rights as her mother years ago. Zina, you weren't thinking about her when you were out there in those streets prostituting now were you?" Nana saw me come in the door and she used that opportunity to hurt momma. However, momma didn't see me. Her back was facing me, and Nana knew this. "That's right Zina, you didn't tell your daughter about your profession, did you? How you made your money as a whore and that is why I kicked you out. Did you tell Zoya how you ran off with your pimp and left her in an abandoned building for dead? How fortunate that the good Lord showed your father a vision that you were in trouble. I remember it as if it was yesterday.' Nana sat in the chair. "It was raining really hard that evening. It was the worst storm that we'd ever seen in Macon. Your father was determined to find you because the Lord had commanded him to do so. Joe hit every crack house looking for you. He got lucky and hit the right crack house. Apparently, you'd left Zoya with another crack head and she was about to sell your daughter for a hit. Your father's authority in God frightened the exchange and they dropped her and ran for their dear life. If your father didn't get there in time we would have never had Zoya. Did you think about that? No, you were so ungrateful all you thought about was yourself." Nana enjoyed throwing momma's secret in my face. I slammed the door shut behind me and momma jumped. Momma turned to see the shocked look on my face. "Well go ahead and tell Zoya the truth," Nana gloated. Momma replied in defeat, "You've already done that momma, therefore, there is nothing more to tell." Momma walked away and slammed my room door behind her.

I couldn't move. I was in shock. Hearing those lies about momma. It couldn't be true. Tears fell down my face, I could only look at Nana with disgust. I was headed towards my room and Nana grabbed my arm to stop me. Nana looked down in my face and said, "It's best you know the truth child. As the Bible says the truth will set you free." I snatched my arm from her grip and I answered Nana in a calm force, "Yes Nana, the truth should set us free, but the truth broke my heart today." I walked past Nana and went into my room to find Momma sitting on the bed with the window up, smoking her cigarette. I could see that she was embarrassed, hurt and broken. Momma flicked her cigarette out the window and then looked in my face. Momma sighed and said, "There is more to the story than you know Zo. It didn't go down like that. Let's get out of here because I want to be honest with you." Momma stood up to put on her coat and passed me my coat from the closet. "Momma where are we going?" I asked. She looked at me with sad eyes and said, "I'm taking you to meet my past." We both came out of my room with our coats on, and saw Grandpa Joe talking to Nana.

"Where do you think you're going Zoya? Take off that coat and go back into your room. Now!" I stood behind momma in fear of what Nana might do to me. "Mary," I had never heard momma call Nana by her first name, "I'm taking my daughter for a walk." Nana was angry now. "You will do no such thing. She is not your daughter she is mine," and Nana turned to me. "Zoya go in your room and take off that coat." Grandpa Joe stood up so hard that the chair hit the floor with a loud clash. We all looked at him in shock. "Mary leave them be!" Grandpa was angry. I'd never seen him angry before. Nana was taken back by Grandpa's demeanor. She said, "Joseph Walsh how dare you?" "I dare it woman. I had enough of the devil running my home. It's time that we all make things right. Here Zina take the car keys and you tell Zoya about your past. It's better she hears it from you because you lived it." Nana walked away, went in her room and slammed her bedroom door. She slammed the door so hard that all the pictures of our family fell off the wall and the glass inside the frame shattered. I went to clean it up and Grandpa Joe said, "No Zoya. The shattered glass represents us as a family. It's best that I clean it up." Momma kissed Grandpa Joe on the cheek and said, "Thank you Daddy." Momma grabbed my hand and we left the house. We drove around for what felt like hours and then we stopped on a block that gave me chills. I turned to momma and said, "What is this place?" Momma replied, "This is my past Zo." Momma turned the car off and removed her coat. "Zo, what I have to share is the truth." I removed my coat and braced myself for what I was about to hear.

MY FIRST LOVE

Mary Jo Wilson was finally married. Mary was not married to any man, but to the most prominent, successful man in Macon, Georgia. Joseph was well respected in the community, a passionate lawyer and now a great Overseer/Pastor of Friendly Baptist Church. Mary felt like she hit the lottery or something. Mary remembered when Joseph first entered her daddy's home on that cool September month. Daddy summoned Joseph to our home to help with legal matters pertaining to our land. Daddy inherited land from my great-grandmother and the white folks tried to trick daddy into signing away the deed. Mr. Walsh and his legal team saved our land, and he also won my heart.

A few weeks went by, I couldn't stop thinking about Mr. Walsh. When I closed my eyes I saw his smile, and green eyes that danced when he looked at me, and how nice he smelled. I guess what really won my heart was how he loved the Lord. Mr. Walsh always opened up in prayer before he discussed a deal and closed out in prayer believing God that the deal was sealed. Mr. Walsh would quote the scripture Isaiah 55:11, "So shall my word be that go forth out of my mouth; it shall not return unto me void, but it shall accomplish that which I please, and it shall prosper in the thing whereto I sent it, knowing that it was well with the Lord." On that day, daddy was complaining about headaches and Mr. Walsh laid his large hands on daddy's head. In his authoritative tone he said, "In the name of Jesus be healed and Devil I evict you from taking space in Mr. Wilson's head. Go now! In Jesus name and he concluded Amen." We all said, "Amen" in agreement. Mr. Walsh prayed heaven down, and daddy never suffered another headache.

What woman in her right mind wouldn't love a man like that? I really missed this man and I couldn't help how I was feeling about him. I was sitting on the porch swing thinking about Mr. Walsh again. I was so lost in my thoughts that I didn't see daddy emerge from the house heading towards his truck. Daddy turned to me and said, "Mary Jo, I'm going into town would you like to go with me baby girl?" I denied his request to go for a ride because I was feeling so empty. Daddy sensed my despair and said, "Well I guess you don't want to come with me to see Mr. Walsh." I jumped off the swing as if it had nails in it and my eyes were bulging out of my head. "Daddy are you really going to see Mr. Walsh?" Daddy, smiled at my response and said, "I have to hand him the new deed to register with the state, so I guess you can come along." Before Daddy finished his sentence, I was sitting in the car ready. Daddy put on his hat and shook his head.

As we arrived at Mr. Walsh's office, my hands were sweaty due to my nervousness in seeing him again. We entered Mr. Walsh's law firm and there he was buried behind piles of paper. Mr. Walsh jumped up and knocked over some papers when he saw me enter his office. Daddy and I helped Mr. Walsh pick up the documents from the floor. After we finished picking up the papers, daddy handed his documents to Mr. Walsh. I knew that it was time to leave and I hated the feeling that was coming over me. We got up to leave and Mr. Walsh touched my arm lightly and asked me to have dinner with him later that night. Daddy looked at Mr. Walsh with raised eyebrows. "Mr. Walsh, Mary Jo is a good, church fearing woman of God. I'd like to know what your intentions are with my daughter." In my mind, I didn't care what his intentions were, as long as I was with him. Mr. Walsh looked over to daddy in innocence, he was blushing and said, "Mr. Wilson, I assure you that my intentions are pure Sir." Daddy folded his arms and skeptically looked Mr. Walsh up and down then replied, "Really?" I was mortified. I turned my head so hard that the pin curls dropped from my hair. "Daddy!" Mr. Walsh turned to my father and said, "Mr. Wilson I've been seeking the Lord for a wife," however, Mr. Walsh was looking at me the entire time while speaking to daddy. "I'm in love with Mary and the Lord gave me confirmation that she is the wife for me."

Mr. Walsh turned to my father and said, "She's all I think about Mr. Wilson." Daddy had a big smile on his face and said, "Well I'm sure the Lord heard my prayers too Mr. Walsh." Mr. Walsh looked at daddy with an inquisitive look on his face. "Mr. Wilson, I don't understand Sir?" "Well, I've been seeking the Lord that a good man would take Mary Jo off my hands." Daddy turned his head and winked at me. We all started laughing. Daddy gave us his blessing to be married. I looked over at my beautiful father, and I was so proud of him. Proud of him for standing up to my mommy and fighting to raise me on his own. My dad is my Hero and my King. Now my King is handing me over to my Prince. This is the most magical moment of my life.

Our engagement was the talk of the town, and I was spending more time with Joseph's family due to the fact that I had very little on my side. Joseph's mother's health began to deteriorate over the past few months of our engagement. We were all praying that God would spare her life to see her oldest son get married. Unfortunately, God saw fit to call Ms. Barbara Ann home before we tied the knot. Joseph was devastated by the loss of his mother. Mother Barbara Ann was the only woman that helped me heal through love. Mother Barbara Ann would say, "Find new love through a bitter heart." She would tell me that I was giving those who wounded me, power over the ability to find love – real love. Who would have thought that love could heal old wounds and make you feel loved again? When I thought back over my childhood, I could feel the cold chills going up my spine. My mother was an abusive drunk who tore me down every day. I looked so much like my father that she made sure I was punished for his sins. My father loved my mother, but he couldn't take her drinking. My mother slept around with everyone, and made money doing it. My friends teased me or was angry with me because my mother broke up their parents' home. I knew as soon as I was old enough I was leaving upstate New York, and going south to find my daddy. My mother's profession brought her wealth through her sins. I knew that I wanted nothing to do with it.

THE LAST BREATH

As momma put the car in park, she turned to me and said, "I'm going to tell you the truth on how I ended up here. Let's go Zo, get out of the car." Momma opened up my side of the car, extended her hand for me to take it. I was not comfortable getting out to the car due to the fact that it was dark and raining hard. "Momma, can't we talk from inside of the car?" "Zo, get out of the car girl and stop being a baby," and she laughed. "Now come on baby girl let's go." I rolled my eyes, put my raincoat hood over my head and got out of the car. Momma put me under her umbrella to prevent me from getting wet. Momma's grip was tight, and it made me feel safe, and my fear was gone immediately. "I have a surprise for you Zoya." I smiled and looked up at momma. "What is it?" "Well you have to wait until we sit down and have some hot chocolate, and then I will give it to you." Momma put my surprise in her pocket and took my hand. I couldn't wait to get to the store to talk and get the gift momma had for me. I loved my mother. As we crossed the street talking and laughing, a car with bright head lights stopped in front of us. The lights were blinding our vision from seeing who was behind the car. Suddenly, my fear emerged, and I knew the voice that was calling my name. It was Nana! "Zoya, get in this car now!"

Nana jumped out of the car while the engine was still running and left her door wide open. Momma put me behind her back to protect me from Nana. "Mary, she is my child, and it's time she gets to know me for herself! You will not destroy her life like you destroyed mine!" Nana was upset now and coming towards us. "Zina, you were on drugs, and slept with many men. I didn't put a gun to your head and make you do it. You don't even know who her father is do you? My granddaughter is a bastard, thanks to you." Momma looked down at the ground hurt by Nana's words. Nana continued hurting momma. "You left Zoya for dead in that crack house." Nana was pointing to that abandoned building across the street. "Now you bring my granddaughter back to the druggies to sell her?" Now momma was upset, "Mary, it was because of you that I started smoking. You were intolerable to live with. You had all these Jesus rules, but none of Jesus' love. Did you forget Mary that Jesus is love? No, you wanted biblical scriptures to be the base of our family so that you could control us. Ever since Zion died, you acted as if it was my fault." Nana pointed to momma and was yelling, "Shut your mouth Zina! How dare you bring up my precious baby?" "Precious? He was gay, and you couldn't handle it. You made him a prisoner in our own home, Mother. You made him study scriptures about what Christ hated, and the one thing Christ was you couldn't give it to him and that was love." "How dare you Zina?" Nana started attacking momma. Nana tried to grab me by my hair and momma pushed her. "Mary don't you ever pull my child by her hair again." Nana was upset, and she slapped my mother so hard she hit the floor. I screamed at my Nana to leave my mother alone, but Nana was strong and shoved me really hard. I ended up falling into a puddle of water watching the two women I love fight. Momma got up from the floor and tried her best not to hit Nana back. "Mary, leave me alone. I'm numb to your threats and your physical abuse. You can't hurt me or control me anymore. I will take my daughter tonight. We're leaving for Chicago." Nana stood in momma's way of retrieving me from the puddle I was sitting in. Nana was all in momma's face, "You're not taking my grandchild anywhere." Then Nana shoved momma so hard that the truck didn't see momma. I screamed, "Momma look out!" She turned to look at me. It was over. The truck hit momma so hard that she flew up in the air and landed on top of Grandpa Joe's car. The fall was so hard that the roof of Grandpa Joe's car was completely destroyed.

I ran over to see if momma was ok, and Nana grabbed me to stop me. I pushed Nana so hard that she knew I would not hold back from slapping that demon out of her. I climbed on top of the hood of the car to touch momma's hair. She looked over at me and managed to pull the locket out of her pocket. She handed it to me and said, "I'm sorry Zo," and momma took her last breath. Momma's eyes were open and on her face was peace. Momma was finally free and at peace. I heard this scream come out of me. It sounded like a wounded animal. The rain finally stopped, and I had momma's blood all over my hands, face and clothes. I couldn't talk. Everything was moving in slow motion. I could see Nana running over to me holding me tight, the ambulance took my momma off the car. Grandpa Joe jumped out of the taxi and saw what was going on, and he ran to the ambulance and pulled my mother to his chest, crying. The police pulled him away from Momma's body, but he wouldn't let her go. He was begging God to give him back his daughter. He said, "This is my only daughter, don't take her away from me God. Please don't." Then Grandpa Joe put his hand on his heart and his face looked funny. Grandpa Joe fell on the ground holding his heart. Nana started screaming, and she ran over to Grandpa Joe. The first responders were working on Grandpa Joe's heart. I stood there motionless wondering how this could be happening to me. It started to rain again, and I couldn't move.

Nana and I were riding in the ambulance with Grandpa Joe to the hospital. Everything was moving so fast that I still couldn't speak. Church members were at the hospital comforting Nana. Nana really loved the attention, and I just stared at her in pure hatred. Dr. Grinn entered the hospital and saw me standing there soak and wet. "Zoya, what are you doing here?" Before I could answer, Nana walked over and said, "My daughter was killed in a terrible car accident Dr. Grinn." Dr. Grinn was really concerned and hugged Nana. Watching Nana enjoy the attention was getting on my nerves. Nana was putting on fake tears and then she told Dr. Grinn that Grandpa was in surgery because he had a heart attack. Nana then lightly fainted and everyone swooned around her to give her the aid she needed. Funny how she never mentioned my mother's death only my grandfather's heart attack. Nana murdered my mother, and I will never forgive her Lord. I stood there having an out of body experience watching everything and feeling nothing. Once Dr. Grinn got Nana the medical attention she needed, he turned to me. "Zoya, let's get you out of those wet clothes ok?" I couldn't speak I just nodded my head. As I was walking away with Dr. Grinn, Nana yells for me to come to her. "Where is my Zoya?" Nana, saw me, stretched out her arms and said, "Zoya come to me."

What an actress Nana was. Every one of our church members' eyes were all on me, and then they ushered me to come to my Nana's side. She was crying, touching me, kissing my hand and telling me we were going to be alright. Then Nana said, "And the church members say, 'Amen'. You know Zoya, the Lord moves in mysterious ways and we just have to trust him." I wanted to speak, but couldn't. I wanted to slap her face, but couldn't move. Dr. Grinn, lifted me lightly away from Nana's torture grip and said, "Let me help Zoya get into some dry clothes." Nana suddenly got the strength to sit up from the couch Dr. Grinn placed her on. "Dr. Grinn, that won't be necessary. One of the members of the church can aid my granddaughter in her time of need." Nana turned to Sister Bailey and said, "Sister Bailey can you call home, and get your granddaughter to bring Zoya some clothes." Sister Bailey looked at Nana with a strange look. "First lady Mary, it would take my daughter two hours to get here. Why don't you let the doctor help Zoya I'm sure she's freezing in those wet clothes?" All the members agreed and that pissed Nana off. I managed to get a little smile out of that small victory. Dr. Grinn continued to guide me out of the room and said, "Great! Then it's settled." Dr. Grinn led me to a nurse's station where they provided me with scrubs, sneakers and a sweater to keep me warm. I sat in the spare room, and finally I cried. I remembered my mother's body lying on top of the car covered in blood, was affecting me. I could still hear her laugh and feel her hugs. The last month with my mother was amazing. As I sat there in the dark room crying, I felt Dr. Grinn's hands on my shoulder. He turned on the bedside light and held me in his arms. I cried so much that I soaked his doctor's coat. Dr. Grinn's pager went off and he suggested that I return to my Nana's side. When I entered the waiting area I saw Nana's dislike towards Dr. Grinn. Dr. Grinn, told me that he was going to check on Grandpa Joe and he would be back. Nana stretched out her arms to me, and I turned away and sat on the other side of the waiting room. I just had to talk to God on my own terms.

I left the waiting room and found a chapel. At first, I was praying heaven down. I think I fell asleep and, in this dream, I saw Grandpa Joe. He was really happy, and he looked so young. Grandpa was in this great field and he took my hand and sat me at his feet. Grandpa Joe said, "Hey preacher girl." I answered back, "Hey Preacher Sir." Grandpa became serious and he said, "Zoya one day you're going to preach the gospel to many broken women." Before I could make a joke, Grandpa looked very serious and said, "You are going to have to trust the Lord Zoya, and lean not to your own understanding. For the time has come for me to be with the Lord and for you to carry my legacy." I stood up because I knew where the conversation was going. I said to Grandpa Joe, "Please don't leave me with her." I knelt down and placed my head on his lap. Then I saw two women tell my Grandpa Joe that it was time. One of the women was my mother Zina, and the other woman looked like my great grandmother Barbara Ann. I didn't want them to leave me here, so I shouted, "Take me with you." I looked around for items to take my life so that I could join them. My mother came to me and said, "This is not the way to join us Zoya. Taking your life doesn't get you a seat in heaven, only a place in hell. You have to fulfill your purpose and your calling. For the Lord walks with you. I love you Zoya, and I will be waiting for you." I started to see them fade away. I was screaming, "Don't go Grandpa Joe, and Momma! Wait, please come back." I was awakened out of the dream by Dr. Grinn. Once I looked in his face I already knew that Grandpa Joe said goodbye to me before he departed the earth. I lost two people in one day, momma and Grandpa Joe. The unfortunate thing about this day was it happened to be my birthday.

A NEW BEGINNING

It's been 5 years since the home-going service for momma and Grandpa Joe. What a beautiful service. The members of Greater Love & Peace Baptist Church handled the service in the spirit of excellence. The NAACP was there to honor grandpa with a Proclamation Award for all his years of legal services to the community. There were great speakers and singers. Grandpa Joe looked so handsome in his suit. He looked as if he was taking a nap in that old chair he loved so much at home. As I sat next to Nana, I noticed how strong she was. Nana didn't shed one tear. She was too busy planning, making arrangements, calling people and cooking for the repast. Then I looked over at the other coffin which held my beautiful mother. How peaceful she looked in the dress I picked out for her. I was happy that Nana allowed me to purchase momma's dress. I wanted momma to be dressed in a white gown as the bride going home to Jesus. Nana wanted momma in black, but she was too tired to argue with me. I was glad that she allowed me to make that decision. After all, it was her fault that my mother was in that coffin.

There were so many people in attendance that there was standing room only in the church. It was my turn to go up there and say a few words regarding my mother and grandpa. I heard my name being called, and my feet were moving oh so slow. The pulpit seemed as if it was 100 feet away from me. When I finally had the microphone in my hand and looked out into the audience, I felt their love for me. I began talking about my mother and how much I was going to miss her. As I began to talk about my Grandpa Joe, I felt something come over me. It was like God downloaded a message in me for the people. I began to speak on 2 Corinthians that spoke on trouble not lasting forever. The trouble and sadness that we were faced with, actually helps to produce a glory that vastly outweighs any of them. I read 2 Corinthians 4:17-18, "For our present troubles are small and won't last very long. Yet they produce for us a glory that vastly outweighs them and will last forever. So, we don't look at the troubles we can see now; rather, we fix our gaze on things that cannot be seen. For the things we see now will soon be gone, but the things we cannot see will last forever." As I was moving in the spirit, people were standing to their feet. I opened my mouth and God spoke through me. I didn't know how to turn it off. The musician started to follow me, and I began to come off the pulpit and groan like grandpa. I felt him there with me edging me on, it was like fire shut up in my bones. When God stopped, I stopped, and when I looked around people were shouting and praising God. I looked over to where Nana sat, and she was up shouting and praising God. I'd never seen her do that before. All of a sudden, the spirit of joy was all over me and I dropped the mic and I began to shout as well. It was a beautiful homegoing service, one that changed my life forever.

A few months after Grandpa Joe died the lawyers called Nana and I to the reading of the Will. Grandpa Joe had a lot of investments that he left to momma and because she died, it was passed down to me. When I became 21, I would inherit land, cars, the ministry and college fund of $500,000. I was excited. Nana would oversee my trust fund until I was old enough to manage it. Nana had lots of money as well. The NAACP left Nana with a good amount of money that they raised for Grandpa Joe. Nana was set for life. The lawyer informed Nana that the church was in my name and not hers. This information didn't please Nana and the look on her face showed it. Nevertheless, Nana and my relationship was working out. We were actually getting along, and she allowed me to have a computer and a cell phone. She had no choice, I was 18 and she wanted to know where I was at all times. It took me some time to forgive Nana. When I did, I saw her remorse and she finally broke down. Nana cried in my arms for 3 hours, and I knew I had to forgive her and myself. I think Nana enjoyed me being home with her all the time. I truly believed she allowed me to mourn so long for selfish reasons.

We prayed together more, read scriptures a lot and Nana allowed me to preach on youth Sundays. I really felt closer to God more now than I did since Grandpa Joe was called home. I found comfort in the Word of God, and understood my calling to preach the gospel. Nana bragged about the calling for me to preach and would inspire me to take Grandpa Joe's place on the pulpit. Nana was booking me at every youth service and speaking to the youth throughout the community counsel board. Nana kept my schedule extremely busy since I was 15. Nana wanted me to write books for young people to inspire them on purity. However, I wasn't ready to tell the world that I was 18 and a virgin. Nana had all these plans for my life, but I had plans of my own. I wanted to go to college and become a lawyer like Grandpa Joe.

One day while in school, my guidance counselor, Mrs. Tina, sent for me during my 3rd period class. I was nervous and didn't know why I was summoned to Mrs. Tina's office. I was hoping that Nana was ok. I started to pray inwardly because I couldn't take another death right now. I stood at the door of Mrs. Tina's office afraid to knock. I took a few deep breaths and knocked on her door. Mrs. Tina invited me in and asked me to close the door behind me. I closed the door and she offered me a seat. I watched her lips preparing myself for some horrible news about Nana. Mrs. Tina picked up the phone and told our Assistant Principal Mr. Jewel, that I was in her office. Oh my God now I was really nervous, but I tried to appear reserved and strong. Mr. Jewel walked in the office with a smile on his face, and I could tell that it wasn't as bad as I thought. Mr. Jewel folded his arms and said, "Young lady, we have gotten several calls from universities implying that you were a recipient to receive scholarships and they hadn't heard from you." Ms. Tina chimed in, "Are you crazy young lady? These are well established and accredited schools wanting you Zoya. What's going on? Are you not responding for a reason?" I was left with my mouth open. "Mrs. Tina and Mr. Jewel, I assure you that I have not received any letters at my home. My Nana would have given them to me." Mrs. Tina gave me a copy of the 10 letters from the universities. "Zoya, you have the highest-grade point average in the city of Macon. It is not surprising that these prominent law schools are calling for you." Mrs. Tina knew how I felt about Nana, and she had me respond in her office to the universities. Going forward, I decided to use my school's address, so I wouldn't miss anymore letters.

On my way home, I was furious with Nana for withholding those letters from me. What was she thinking by holding me back? Nana and her control to let me go is on high. I entered the house and I heard Nana's voice on the phone. She seemed upset and when I entered the kitchen I asked, "Nana what's wrong?" Why was I asking her what's wrong and she did me wrong? Nana was upset that a boy name Jordan was calling the house for me. I immediately forgot that I was upset with her. In my excitement, I grabbed Nana by the hand and wanted to know what he said. Nana pulled her hand away from me in disgust and said, "I told him never to call this house again." I was taken back by her rudeness and disappointed in her behavior to keep me to herself. "Nana, you have no right to treat Jordan like that. I like Jordan and if I didn't leave my phone home he would have never called this house." Nana was shocked and grabbed my arm so tightly that it hurt. "You've been seeing a boy and talking to him behind my back Zoya? Why would you do something like that to me?" "Nana, I'm 18 now, I'm supposed to be liking someone other than you." Nana went into the room and returned with the Bible. "Zoya you can repent now from all your wicked thoughts. The Bible talks about wicked imaginations, the Lord will forgive you. Boys will ruin you and make you sin before God. You have to stay pure that is how God wants his servants to be, pure." "Speaking of repentance, Nana is there something you would like to share with me regarding letters from universities that were addressed to me?" "Zoya, I did that for your own good. We don't need no more lawyers in the family the Will of God called you to preach, and preaching is what you will do." "Nana, correct me if I'm wrong, but God gives us a free will or did you forget that? I've already replied to the universities and I'm accepting a few of their scholarships. I want to travel outside these four walls and your need to make me your only companion. You can't control me Nana not anymore." Nana pointed her finger at me and said, "You will honor me as the Bible says and respect my wishes over your life. I know what the Lord wants for you." I was shocked at her behavior. "Nana stop it! You don't know anything about me outside of preaching. I'm in love with Jordan and I have been in a relationship with him for the past 6 months. We're in love Nana and I want you to be happy for me." Nana walked over to make her some tea. I couldn't stop smiling knowing that Jordan was persistent in finding me.

Next thing I knew I was ducking from the kettle that was being thrown at me. The kettle missed me, but made a hole in the wall and made me look at Nana in shock. The last time she hit me with something I was in the hospital in a coma. Nana spoke, and it wasn't her voice at all. Nana turned to me and her eyes looked like the devil was in her. "You're just like your mother! She let some boy enter her life and crawl his filthy thing between her legs. Once you let them demons inside of you, seven more enter. Your mother changed." Nana shook her finger at me. "Once she gave up her gift, she started smoking, drinking and talking back to me. Your grandfather never saw nothing wrong. He claimed it was a phase and she would grow out of it. After she broke up with the love of her life, more boys began to enter her until I didn't even recognize her. She started wearing that paint on her face, sexy undergarments and 6 inch heals like a whore." I stopped her in mid-sentence. "How dare you call my mother names? You killed her Nana. You pushed her into oncoming traffic because she was trying to tell me to get away from you."

Now it was Nana's turn to be angry. "Zoya, as long as you live in my house you will do as I say." Now Zoya was upset and she approached Nana in boldness until she was eye to eye with her. "I will leave your house this day, and I will never return." Nana became physical and pushed me so hard I fell on the seat on top of the kitchen table and it broke. Nana was on top of me and said, "If you leave this house you will get nothing from me. Remember I oversee your trust fund and you won't get a dime, if I find you unfit. Remember you have three more years until you're 21." "Nana, I will go with nothing in my pockets, but I will have freedom and independence. Now get off of me." I went into my room and packed a few things in my suitcase, and Nana ran behind me.

As I was packing clothes into my suitcase, Nana was removing them out of the suitcase. "You're not going anywhere," Nana said. Nana grabbed my hair and we began to fight. I let Nana hit me, but I would not hit her back. I would block her blows and push her off me while I continued to grab what I could, and run out the house. I couldn't take it no more. I promised Grandpa Joe that I would never tell Nana what I knew, but she pushed me. Nana screamed, "I am your grandmother and you will do as I say." I knew if I let Nana know the secret it would probably kill her, and I was well with it. "Technically Nana, you're not my real grandmother." Nana's face was turning white. "Grandpa Joe told me that you couldn't have babies, and God blessed you with Zion, your son. You were obsessed with Zion to the point that you wouldn't let Grandpa hold his own son. It was all about you and Zion. Grandpa Joe needed his wife by his side and you rejected him. You treasured Zion because your mother made you abort your first born. I know how the doctors said you could never conceive again." "Shut up Zoya," said Nana. But Zoya was on a role now. "Nana you were pregnant by your mother's boyfriend, and your mother hated you for it. She mistreated you and took your daughter out of your body. When you had Zion, you were selfish, and you didn't want to share him with anyone, not even Grandpa Joe. You left Grandpa Joe lonely and longing for your love. Grandpa Joe told me the secret; he had an affair with Deaconess Jones. Deaconess Jones got pregnant a year later with momma, and you were furious. You hated Grandpa Joe for what he did, and you never slept with him again as punishment. Deaconess Jones died in childbirth and had no family, so Grandpa Joe had you raise my momma. You mistreated her since she was a little girl because she didn't come out of your womb. You left momma in her diaper for hours stinking until Grandpa Joe came home from work. My mother Zina, was so beautiful that she stole the shine from her brother, and you resented that. You resented that Grandpa Joe's love child got all the attention, and was so sweet. Grandpa Joe told me how hurt you were when you found out that Zion, your son, would wear momma's clothes. You would beat the Word of God in him until he felt that God didn't love him."

"Zoya, shut your mouth. These are lies." Nana was sitting on the bed with tears rolling down her face. I couldn't stop so I continued releasing what was built up in me for years. "Nana, Grandpa Joe said that when Zion was 15 years old, he had problems that you wouldn't see. You made Zion sleep in the bed with you until he was 15 years of age, and he was interested in girls. You never let Zion leave your side until one day he was kicked out of school from forcibly touching boys. That's when you started to home school him. Grandpa Joe said you thought you could fix Zion wanting boys, so you allowed him to peek at my mother so that he could get some sort of arousal. One day Grandpa Joe went upstairs to check on momma and he found Zion on top of her. Zion was 18 years old, and my mother was 17 years old. Grandpa pulled Zion off my mother and while he was beating him, you came in between them. You were accusing my mother of seducing Zion. Calling her a whore like her mother. That is when momma found out you weren't her real mother. Eventually, Zion ran away from home, and years later he was in jail for raping little boys. Grandpa Joe said Zion hung himself in jail because he suffered the same fate of being raped while in prison. See Nana, my mother wasn't a whore like you said. Your son had mental issues because of you, and he raped my mother and it produced me." Nana slapped me so hard that I hit the floor and so did she. I looked over at Nana and she was clutching her heart having a heart attack. I felt really bad because I let the devil use me. "God please forgive me." I grabbed the phone to call 911, and they arrived in 20 minutes. Off to the hospital we went.

FIGHTING BACK

Nana suffered a major heart attack and was hospitalized for three months. When word spread around the church, the senior members of the congregation really mistreated me. The Elders wanted to know what I said to Nana that would cause her to have a heart attack. As if a human being can cause someone's heart to go bad. The way they stared at me when they visited Nana made me go into a deep stage of depression. I had no one to talk to. Grandpa Joe and momma were no longer here to protect me. Nevertheless, the members of the church wanted to know our family business and Nana made me promise to take our family secrets to my grave. I can see Nana's face and hear her words "what goes on in our house, stays locked in the house." Therefore, I had to create a story that would satisfy the Elders and the seniors of the church. I told the church that I tried to run away and that broke Nana's heart. It made me look like the bad guy and Nana loved the story. As a matter of fact, Nana added more to the story to make her become more of the victim. Nana won again.

I finally graduated from Macon High School with honors, however, I turned down the offers for scholarships. Nana needed me home to take care of her after her heart attack. I also ended my relationship with Jordan, and Nana was very happy that I did. Jordan on the other hand was not pleased at all, and he called me all kinds of names. I was happy that I broke up with Jordan. I had never been called such ungodly names before, not even by Nana on her worst day. Jordan called me a stupid Jesus freak, church girl, and told me my first intercourse would be with a cross. Wow! Really Jordan? I was so over him. I tried to explain that my obligation was to God first, but it only made him angrier. If you asked me, I really believed that our family had turned Jordan off in regards to church. Well, no need to cry over a river that's damned Nana would always say. I just threw myself into ministry and focused on preaching engagements. I also enrolled in a religious community college in the area. I guess God was punishing me for my sins and I deserved it.

A year went by and Nana purchased a new home for us to live in. Nana said that the old house had too many memories of

Grandpa Joe and she had to move on. I really agreed with Nana on this move. I saw Grandpa Joe everywhere in our old home and it was becoming depressing. Nana purchased a four-bedroom house with 3 bathrooms, 14 acres of land, swimming pool and a large basement in Stapleton, GA. In the back of my mind I felt that Nana bought this new home to keep me as a prisoner. She kept saying that when I got married, my husband and children would inherit the home she purchased for us. That only indicated that not only was I going to remain in bondage, but so would my family. We lived further into the deep part of Georgia and I couldn't understand why Nana brought a home with nothing but woods as our neighbors. Although my room was equipped with my own bathroom and walk in closet. Nana and I had our own offices in the house with the latest technology in it. Nana had security cameras installed around the house especially outside my room. It was a bit uncomfortable to have Nana watch my every move. Nevertheless, I was grateful to have my own car to come and go as I pleased. Which was only school, church, driving Nana around and speaking engagements. Nana hired workers to manage the house, cook and clean our mini-mansion. We had no time to cook, shop or clean the big house Nana purchased. Nana and I never discussed the incident leading to her heart attack. Therefore, we just pretended that it never happened.

I was invited to speak at Macon Grace Fire Baptist Church in two weeks. Macon Grace was one of the largest churches in the community. Prior to my speaking engagement with Senior Pastor Wilbur Barnes, Nana and I were invited to their home for brunch. It was an hour drive from Stapleton to Macon, but it felt good coming back home. The Barnes lived in one of the mansions in Macon, and Pastor Barnes and Grandpa were really good friends in college. Nana and I arrived at the Barnes' house at 2pm Saturday afternoon. It was extremely warm for the month of April and it seemed as if Summer was in the air. Pastor Barnes and his wife were the greatest hosts to Nana and myself. Pastor Barnes wanted to know if God had given me a word for his house. I'd mentioned that the Lord did give me a word, although I was extremely nervous sitting in front of this great man of God. Pastor Barnes' sermons are all over the local network stations and he had over 2,000 members in his church. Pastor Barnes had celebrity connections, and he sat on the board of directors at the NAACP. Therefore, I was certainly intimidated by this great man of God sitting before me. Pastor Barnes led me into his grand office with law and religious books surrounding his wall. Once inside the office we entered another room which Pastor Barnes called the sitting room. The sitting room was as big as my room and the walk-in closet put together. As I took my seat, Pastor Barnes led us into a prayer, and I felt the power of God immediately.

As I began to share with Pastor Barnes that the Lord had given me the scripture Isaiah 6:8. "Then I heard the voice of the Lord, saying, 'Whom should I send? Who will go for Us?' Then I said, 'Here am I. Send me!'" Pastor Barnes was fully engaged in what I had to say. I didn't see Pastor Barnes anymore, I opened my mouth and the Lord spoke through me. I wasn't afraid, and I felt God with me as I spoke. I said with such authority, "Pastor Barnes my topic for consideration is Messengers Needed for the Shift." Pastor Barnes smiled and crossed his arms over his chest. "Zoya, can you elaborate a little for me," said Pastor who was intrigued. "Yes, Pastor. I remembered a scenario while working part-time in the college office. An announcement came from the top in regards of lay-offs, and no one wanted to deliver the message. The message wasn't popular, some would be offended, and the messenger would not be liked. Who would deliver this message that would shift the atmosphere? I immediately thought, can God trust us as a messenger to deliver his word that will shift the atmosphere? Who can he send to be truthful and bring deliverance to a lost generation?" Pastor Barnes was applauding and praising God at the same time. "Young lady you're definitely the messenger for this assignment. I won't let you expound on too much information I'd like to hear it when it's delivered. However, I like where you're going with this."

After further mentoring with Pastor Barnes he was well pleased that I was in tune with the vision of his church. Pastor Barnes and I emerged to the living room where Nana and First Lady Barnes were seated. Pastor Barnes caught the two ladies in a full-fledged conversation of gossip. Pastor Barnes cleared his throat to let Nana know that he was finished his mentoring session with me. Nana jumped up when she heard Pastor Barnes clear his throat because she was caught gossiping. When Nana saw the smile on

Pastor Barnes' face she was pleased. First lady Barnes saw that her husband was pleased with the mentoring that she immediately stood up with her hands on her chest smiling at her husband. Everyone was happy except me. Here I was, 19 years old, and never kissed a boy or knew the love of a man. But I was anointed, called, handpicked by the Lord and lonely. I always wondered if the scripture in Ephesians 3:1 where Paul shared that he was a prisoner of Christ Jesus for the sake of the unbelievers. First Lady pulled me out of my thoughts and invited us to stay for dinner. I just wanted to go home and lock myself in my room. I started chatting online with a man named Ollie, who had been such a great friend to me. We'd been talking for 6 months, and I was really starting to fall for him. Ollie grew up in a religious home just like me, and he really understood me. However, I knew there was no way of getting around or out of this invitation. The grown-ups were engrossed in a conversation concerning my life that I needed to get away from them.

I politely excused myself to the bathroom where I cried behind closed doors. I stayed there for a good five minutes. I'm sure everyone thought I was making number two. Finally, I washed my face and dried my eyes. I had to prepare myself for the rest of the evening talking about nothing else, but the Lord. Don't get me wrong; I didn't mind talking about the goodness of the Lord. However, I wished I had more young people that were like me, young and anointed. I opened the door and there stood this handsome young man leaning against the wall with his arms folded. He said, "Should I hold my nose from the smell?" I was annoyed at his rudeness and I coldly said, "If I had pooped you certainly would've smelled it." He looked like Pastor, but he was definitely a rebel, I could see it in his heart.

"I'm sorry we got off on the wrong smell, my name is Mesh." He extended his hand. I relaxed and shook his hand to introduce myself. Before I could introduce myself, Mesh said, "So you must be the fireball preacher Zoya." I was somewhat annoyed. I felt that he was mocking me. "You can call me Zoya minus the fireball preacher please." Mesh smiled at me and said, "My bad Zoya minus the fireball preacher." He was intrigued. "My father sent me to retrieve you, and to make sure you're ok." Zoya felt bad about snapping at him. Mesh smiled, and held out his arm to escort her to his father and guest. My father named me after Meshack in the Bible, so all my friends call me Mesh. Zoya smiled and said, "I see." When Mesh and Zoya walked in arm and arm, Nana froze in her seat. Pastor introduced his son Mesh to Nana. Pastor Barnes was pleased that Zoya and Mesh were hitting it off.

Pastor Barnes smiled at Nana and said, "Mary maybe your granddaughter can rub off some of her anointing on my son." First Lady and everyone laughed, except Nana. Mesh shook his head at his father and said, "Dad you got jokes right?" First Lady suggested that Mesh show Zoya around the house while dinner was being prepared. Zoya smiled happily just to be around another young person. Pastor Barnes said, "You kids go on and enjoy each other's company." Nana was upset. I could tell by the look on her face. Nana stood up quickly and said, "I have to decline dinner because I have such a headache Pastor Barnes." Zoya knew what this was about. Nana didn't have a headache. Nana didn't want her with the Pastor's son or any boy. Zoya looked down and was prepared to take Nana home. Pastor Barnes said, "Nonsense, you can stay the night and rest your head. Let Zoya have a great evening with some young people. A few of my family members are coming over and after all, young people need young people." Nana stood up and started walking towards me so that she could grab me and leave. Nana said, "That's very nice of you, but I insist that we leave now." "Zoya, let's go," Nana said. Pastor Barnes stood up from his chair and said, "Mary, as your Overseer you dare to disrespect my hospitality?" Nana knew she could not win this fight and I was so happy that someone stood up to her. First Lady Barnes touched Nana's arm and led her to the guest room where she would be staying for the night. Pastor Barnes looked over at me and said, "So go on young people, enjoy your night." I smiled and Pastor Barnes winked his eye at me. I could tell that Pastor Barnes knew Nana's control over me, and he insisted that I have a good time with my peers.

Pastor Barnes' daughter Shelly arrived, she was about my age, and a few of their cousins arrived as well. The house was so busy with people, laugher and music. Having dinner with the Barnes' family was so much fun that I ignored Nana's stare. For the first time in a long time I was laughing, and it felt good. Nana sat at the dinner table watching and judging all of them, I could tell. Nana was careful not to offend Pastor Barnes for he kept a watchful eye on her. All the young people were going to the mall for ice cream, and they invited me to join them. Shelly looked me over and said, "Hey Zo you're overdressed for the mall. I have some shorts and flip flops you can borrow." I smiled thinking, "Oh my God! I get to wear shorts," and then she looked over at Nana. Nana's eyes bore into her to show her disapproval. Pastor Barnes gave the ok for us to go to the mall. Pastor Barnes mentioned to Mesh and Shelly to be home by 12am and no later. Mesh and Shelly agreed, and off from the dinner table we went.

When Zoya entered Shelly's room she was in awe of the posters that were hanging on her wall. She had Biggie Smalls, P-Diddy and Faith Evans. Zoya looked at Shelly and asked, "Is your dad ok with these secular unsaved people on your wall?" Shelly smiled and said, "The only person that is unsaved, is your grandmother." They both laughed at the same time. Shelly said, "My dad is not like that. He understands young people because he remembers that he was once a young person. I just can't blast my music in the house when my father is in the house that would show disrespect." Shelly found the shorts buried in her uncleaned room. "Ah ha! Zoya here are the shorts, tee-shirt and sandals you can borrow." Zoya put on the garments and then she looked in the mirror. "Wow!" She looked amazing and she turned side to side admiring her figure. Shelly laughed, "Is this your first time getting to see what you look like from the waist down?" Zoya laughed, "yes and no." Shelly looked at her for a long time and responded. "Damn, girl you going to have my brother drooling all over you." Zoya smiled shyly, and then they both laughed like school girls.

Mesh was pulling his motorcycle out of the garage when he caught sight of Zoya coming down the driveway. Mesh couldn't move, he was in total shock that Zoya was this beautiful outside of her potato sack clothes. Zoya's, heart started beating really fast seeing that look on Mesh's face. As they all stood together, Shelly had to hit Mesh to get him to speak. Shelly laughed, "Mesh doesn't Zo look beautiful?" Mesh took Zoya's hand and kissed it. Mesh managed to say, "Zoya I know why your grandmother dresses you down?" Zoya was puzzled and said, "why do you say that?" Mesh walked around her, examining her body. "Girl you're very sexy!" Mesh said. Zoya was blushing. She never saw herself as sexy, and she was enjoying this kind of attention. Off to the mall the teenagers went. Zoya on Mesh's bike and Shelly in the car with her cousins.

The next morning Nana sat up in her bed looking around the room for Zoya. Nana was ready to leave the Barnes' house immediately. However, Zoya was not in her bed and Nana begin to panic. Nana got out of bed and fell to the floor screaming, "My heart! Help, my heart!" First Lady Barnes was in the kitchen preparing breakfast and heard Nana's screams. Shelly woke-up Zoya, who fell asleep in her room after talking all night, it's your grandmother. Zoya jumped out of her bed and ran downstairs where everyone was. Pastor Barnes was praying for Nana, but she didn't want God. She wanted me. Once I turned the corner to enter the guest room, Nana saw me. Nana saw the lip gloss on my lips, the mascara on my eyes and how loose my hair was. Nana's look on her face revealed to me that I would never see the Barnes again. I knew once back home in Stapleton, the speaking engagement would be cancelled unknowingly. I knew that I would never see this family again. Nana insisted that I drove her home so that she could have her doctor make a house call. Pastor Barnes interceded and said, "Ok Mary, as you wish." Pastor turned to his wife and said, "please see that Mary has her breakfast in bed before her journey. The rest of us will have our meal in the garden." Pastor Barnes turned to Nana and said, "I insist you get rest and prepare for your hour's journey." Nana could say nothing but, "Thank you Pastor," in a very annoyed voice. Pastor Barnes turned to Shelly and said, "Take Zoya upstairs so that you can shower and prepare for breakfast." Shelly smiled, "yes daddy. Come on Zo I have a summer dress you can wear." Off the girls went per the instructions of Pastor Barnes.

We entered the garden to have breakfast and to my surprise Nana was sitting there in yesterday's clothes. Nana was shocked that my hair was not in the ponytail bun she made me wear all the time. The summer dress I wore had no sleeves, so my arms were exposed, and the lip gloss that I was wearing made my lips look beautiful. Pastor Barnes and First lady Barnes complimented me on how beautiful I looked. Nana pretended not to notice, and sat there quiet and still. I sat between Mesh and Shelly. The entire time we kept talking and laughing. Finally, breakfast was over, and Nana and I were preparing to leave. Pastor Barnes escorted Nana to the car making sure she was alright, and then he closed her side of the door behind her. I was saying good-bye to Shelly and Mesh, and gave them both a hug. I was going to miss them greatly. Mesh had his arm around my waist and walked me to the car. Mesh kissed me on the cheek and said good bye to Nana. Nana pretended to have a coughing attack just so that she didn't have to respond back to Mesh. Pastor Barnes walked on my side of the car and said, "Keep the fire burning inside of you young lady." Pastor Barnes held my face in his hands and said, "You're indeed a different type of church girl." Normally, I would get upset when I heard that term "church girl," but this time I felt it when Pastor Barnes said it. I jumped in his arms and held him tight. Tears were flowing down my face for I knew I would never see him again.

Nana was silent as we drove home, and I welcomed her silence. I was thinking about Mesh, and my first kiss with a boy was amazing. The wind was blowing my hair and I felt free and in love. I pulled into the gas station to get gas while Nana sat in complete silence. As I was paying for gas, there were two gentlemen calling me beautiful and asking me my name. I didn't know what to make of it. I was getting attention and I was enjoying it. Nana sat in silence saying nothing and I felt for the first time beautiful.

I pulled up to the driveway and Nana got out of the car without my help. I knew she wasn't sick, she was being manipulative. I went to my room and fell asleep. I woke up to Nana banging on my door and I got up to open it. She was looking around my room for something. I asked Nana what she was looking for? Nana said, "A boy?" "A boy?" I responded. "Really Nana?" I sat on my bed waiting for her dramatic behavior to emerge. Nana started yelling at me indicating that my behavior was ungodly at the Barnes' house. Nana informed me that the committee had an emergency meeting and their cutting ties with Pastor Barnes. I wasn't surprised by Nana's actions, and I expected her to behave immaturely. When Nana didn't get the response she expected from me, that is when she started putting me down. I left my room and headed towards the kitchen to get something to eat. I wasn't going to argue with her so that if she had another heart attack that I wouldn't get blamed for it. Nana was becoming increasingly angry because I would not respond to her verbal abuse. I took her blows the way Jesus took his beating.

After 10 hours of taking Nana's verbal tongue I went to my room and prepared for bed. I prayed to God and asked him to remember me. "Lord, please I know you're there looking down on me. Is there any way you can silence Nana from hurting me? Thank you, Lord." Finally, I fell asleep. I woke up and saw that Nana removed the door to my room, so that she could enter without knocking or catch me with a boy in my room. Still, I wouldn't touch it and I didn't care anymore. I was in love with Mesh. After my shower, I got dressed and prepared for school as usual. When I entered the garage, my car was gone. A man appeared, drove up to the driveway, and got out of the car. I was a little uncomfortable with him. Nana entered the garage and said, "Meet Noel, he will be your personal driver that I hired to take you to school, mall, food shopping and then right back home. Zoya, this is for your own good so that you don't end up like your mother."

That did it! My mother, all the memories I buried started to come back to me. I felt a rage that I hadn't felt in years. I ran back into the house and went to put on the dress Shelly gave me. I removed the bun and let down my hair. I also had make-up form Shelly and I put on that lip gloss. Well if she keeps calling me a whore I might as well own up to the name. When I returned to the garage the driver Noel's eyes bulged open and Nana looked to see what he was staring at. It was me! Yes me! "Where are you going dressed like that Zoya. Get back in the house and change your clothes this instant." Now it was my turn to yell at Nana. "I'm sorry Nana, if you're going to call me a whore I might as well dress like one." Nana was in my face pointing that finger of hers. Nana said, "You will go into that house or I will contact the lawyer and let him know that your mental behavior is in question to obtain the rights to your grandfather's money." I went into the house changed my clothes and was driven to school. Finally, I just gave into Nana.

Mesh came by a few times to see me with little success. Nana turned him away from seeing me by telling Mesh that I didn't want to see him. Mesh wouldn't give up, and Nana finally call the law on him. Pastor Barnes was really upset with Nana and decided to pull me from speaking at his church. I knew that's what Nana wanted more than anything in the world. One night I was sleeping, and I was awakened by a sound hitting my window. I got up and looked out the window and there was Mesh. I was pleased that he wasn't the type to be scared off by Nana. Mesh gave me a cell phone so that we could connect with each other. I was so thankful to God for sending Mesh in my life. Nana had control of the cellular plan we shared. Nana had access to my phone, pictures and text messages, by telling the service provider that I was a minor. Mesh and I would text every day on the phone, and I was able to contact Ollie as well. Ollie had been encouraging me to leave Nana and come to New York.   After months of praying, fasting and seeking God in my situation. Nana finally put the doors to my room back on the hinges. A year later, I graduated from seminary school at the top of my class. I was ready to go away to college to get away from Nana, however, my money wasn't coming until I was 21. I was secretly applying to some law schools outside of Georgia. I needed to be as far away from Nana as I could get.

Later that night, Nana entered my room with a full itinerary of speaking engagements that she scheduled for the summer. I didn't know how to tell her that I had another plan in mind. Nana was going on and on about how she worked hard getting me these engagements. Finally, I stood up and said, "Nana I'm not speaking at anyone's church. I want to go away to college." Nana disregarded my statement and said, "You will do as I say Zoya. I know what's good for you." I prayed, and in all the boldness I could muster up I said, "I'm not going."

Nana got up and grabbed me by my hair and started pulling it so hard I thought my brain was coming out. I managed to fight her off this time. I pushed Nana off me and she slapped me so hard that my ear started ringing.   I was angry, and I slapped her back unintentionally. Nana was so surprised that I hit her that she went in the kitchen to get a knife. Nana was so enraged that her eyes were large, and she said that she would cut that defiant demon out of me. I pleaded with Nana to put the knife down, but she insisted that she would take my life before I could own it for myself. Nana knew how to fight dirty and she was poking the knife towards me.

I had to think fast, and fear was gripping my thoughts. Nana came after me and I hit her on top of her head with a vase. It smashed to pieces on Nana's head and she passed out. There was blood coming out of Nana's head and I screamed.

The servants ran in and saw Nana on the floor and they called the cops. Noel the driver ran to me and gave me the keys to the car. I was shocked, and he said, "Kid this is your turn to break free. Take it and get out of here I will stall the cops." Noel was shouting at me. As I proceeded out the door, I turned to take one last looked at Nana on the floor. Nana wasn't moving, and I knew that my life would never be the same. "Oh my God!" I thought to myself, "she's dead." I realized that I had no money and I ran upstairs to Nana's room. I could hear Noel screaming at me to hurry up. I knew where Nana kept her emergency money. I keep hearing the scriptures "thou shall not steal," I was already convicted of Nana's murder. I thought to myself, one more crime added and I'm sure God is sending me straight to hell. Noel was screaming at me, "hurry up Zoya!" I appeared at the top of the stairs shoving the money in my jeans. Once at the bottom of the stairs I hugged Noel, took his keys and headed towards the door. With tears in my eyes, I opened the door and ran out into the rain. Never looking back, I knew what was ahead of me would change my life drastically. "New York City, ready or not, here I come."

THE LIFE OF A CALLED GIRL

When I arrived in New York, Ollie met me at Penn Station, and I immediately ran into his arms hugging him. I broke down and cried because I thought I killed my grandmother. Ollie assured me that he would take care of me, and not to worry because he had lawyers that could help me. We arrived at Ollie's house. He had a mansion in Queens that they called Jamaica Estates. I had no idea Ollie was rich until I found out later how he made his money. Ollie took good care of me for the first month that I lived with him, and never asked for anything in return. He would call me "church girl" because I was always praying. One day Mesh called me to see if I was okay, and we talked for a little while. Mesh told me that Nana was ok, and she told the police that I was only defending myself. Nana admitted that she came after me with a knife. Therefore, no charges were pressed against me, and I could come back home. However, I didn't want to go back home. I tried to explain to Mesh and that I really loved New York. I mentioned that I was going to go to Law School in New York. Mesh was upset. I told Mesh that I would always love him, but I wasn't returning to Georgia.

After I hung up the phone, Ollie entered my room. His spirit was different. A side I'd never seen before. He was walking around my room asking me questions about my phone call with Mesh. I asked him if he was listening to my phone conversation. Ollie had a dangerous smile, and it made me very uncomfortable. I began to tell him that Mesh was a very good friend that I loved, who helped me during my difficult times with my grandmother. I also shared that my grandmother was alive, and no charges were pressed against me. Ollie said, "And you're planning to go to college?" I smiled "yes." Ollie said, "I have other plans for you Zoya, and it has nothing to do with college." "What do you mean? Ollie you're scaring me?" Ollie smiled and said, "that is a good thing. Most of my girls fear me." "Your girls? You have daughters?" Ollie smiled "yes you can say that I have daughters. However, they work for me. How do you think I managed to get this beautiful house? Let me help you my dear, I run a million-dollar escort service. I really like you, and I'm going to have you as one of my favorite girls."

Ollie opened the door and called out names: "Tasha, Rain, Ginger and Spice come in here and meet your new sister." The girls emerged in the room and they all looked so beautiful. Zoya was so afraid that she couldn't move. Zoya begged Ollie, "please don't do this to me. May the Lord God touch your heart." Ollie interrupted her and said, "Shut up, Church Girl." He turned to his girls and said, "prep her for me. I will be back to take her virginity. Her cries to the Lord her God does not affect me, but turns me on more. It will be my pleasure to break her open myself." He closed the door behind him. Zoya immediately tried to run out the door behind Ollie, but there was a big white guy with a lot of muscles and a gun. Zoya closed the door and gripped herself tightly and began to cry.

Tasha walked over to her and hugged her, Rain went into the bathroom to prepare her bath. Ginger went to the closet to pick her out an outfit to wear to dinner, and Spice was jealous of Zoya. Tasha said, "Listen Zoya there is nothing you can do. Crying is not going to help you. You must face facts that you belong to Ollie now." Rain agreed and said, "listen it will hurt the first time, but if you drink enough wine, you won't feel a thing." Ginger replied, "I will give you some weed. That always helps me out." Spice looked at the girls and said, "are you kidding me? Stop babying the brat. That is what she gets for trusting a complete stranger online and running here for him to save her. Tell her the truth. She's about to become a whore like the rest of us. Her God can't help her now, and why would he help her when he didn't help us when we called on him? Answer that for me church girl."

Zoya said nothing and Spice walked over to her and slapped Zoya across the face so hard that she passed out. Rain grabbed Spice by her arm and said, "are you crazy? Ollie is going to punish you for trying to damage his goods." "I don't care," said Spice. "what is so damn special about her anyway?" Tasha pushed Spice and said, "you are jealous because Ollie has feeling for this girl, and you know it." Ollie entered the room and asked what happened, and no one answered, but he had an idea it was Spice. Ollie approached her and said, "if you touch her again I will put you out on the streets to make money in the slums. Do I make myself clear?" Spice was afraid and knew not to push Ollie. Ollie said, "get her ready for dinner and Spice you're not welcome to join us for dinner. As a matter of fact, leave the room my door bodyguard needs you to do him a freebee." Spice pleaded with Ollie not to give her over to Bruce the bodyguard. The girls knew that Bruce had no respect for women, and he could go for hours just inflicting pain on a woman.

Rain, Tasha and Ginger explained their work and what they did. The three girls were nice to Zoya, but couldn't protect her from the call which she now had to receive. Zoya knew nothing about sex, but was formally educated through the three women who were now her sisters.

Ten years passed, since I picked up the Bible or entered anyone's church. I arrived in New York a virgin and was turned out into the profession of a call girl. I always wondered what was God's assignment in my life? What did God really have planned for me? At this point in my life, it didn't matter anymore. I made my decision and I no longer carried the cross. I worked this game for ten years, made Ollie a lot of money. Nana always said that I was a whore like my momma and her momma before me. I guess it was in my DNA, and I no longer cared. Every now and then I would hear the Word of God stir up in my belly, and I would just shut it off.

One day Ollie called me about a very important man coming to New York on business and needed a date. The man paid Ollie in advance $5,000 for me. These instructions were very simple, I was to wear no make-up, dress in a suit and wear glasses because it was a convention meeting. Ollie sent me in a car to the location and it was at Madison Square Garden. I had a guest pass, but I wasn't sure what this convention was all about. When I arrived through the gates, I saw that a pastor was hosting this religious event. I laughed to myself and said, "God is this some type of joke?" I presented my VIP guest pass to the attendants and they escorted me to a private elevator. The elevator stopped at the VIP level, and a new security guard greeted me to take me where I needed to go. I was escorted to this big room with all these people. I said, "I'm here to see Mr. King." No one judged me because I looked professional. When I entered the room, they were all about to pray and someone said, "Mr. King your guest, Ms. Zoya is here." Mr. King walked over to me and greeted me with a warm handshake. Please join us for prayer Ms. Zoya. I laughed out loud and everyone looked at me.

One lady who looked as if she didn't like me anyway spoke and said, "Ms. Zoya are you afraid of prayer?" Mr. King gave her a look, and she stopped being sarcastic. I had that feeling again in the pit of my belly, and I felt God's presence. It was like coming back to an old relationship that I left a while back. I looked toward the stadium, and the praise and worship team was singing. God was moving in prayer and I felt it. Suddenly, I opened my mouth and said, "I will lead the prayer if you don't mind." I was as shocked as everyone else. Mr. King didn't know what to say, but he felt in his spirit to let me pray.

When Zoya prayed, she provoked the power of God, and it fell in that room. Everyone was praising God, and for the first time Zoya spoke in tongues. Zoya could hear herself speak in this language, but didn't understand what she was saying. She remembered always wanting to speak in tongues and her grandfather would say, "When the power of God falls on you Zo, you will speak in tongues." How could this be that when I'm a sinner, God can still use me? Then Zoya remembered that God is married to the backslider because that is what she was. Zoya fell out under the power of God, and Mr. King left members with her to usher her into the spiritual realm. While Zoya was under the anointing of God she heard him speak to her like never before.

Later that evening Zoya and Mr. King had the opportunity to speak, and Zoya was hoping that she didn't have to sleep with this man after what she experienced on tonight. "Mr. King, you're a man of the cloth and you reached out to a dating/call girl service for a date? I'm confused. You're a Pastor of a mega church and you preach with such fire. Is God aware that you're slipping so to speak?" Mr. King sat back in his chair and said the Bible declares Proverbs 11:30, "he that wins a soul is wise." Zoya interrupts him and says the Bible also says in James 1:3, "Let no man say when he is tempted that it is God tempting him." Mr. King laughed, "Listen, I know that it's an odd thing to do, but when God requests you to do something so unorthodox you do it. God had me request the services of a call girl who was called by him first. God was waiting on you to realize that you're called. I have no intentions of sleeping with you. God's intension was to get you to a service where he could get the glory out of your life. God didn't have me look at a picture the instructions were to send a nice girl and the young man said I have the right one. God knew who had his heart. Nice girl the heart of Christ. Zoya, you may have forgotten who you were, but God didn't forget you." "Then why did he send me to New York to this life?" "Zoya, you have purpose to fulfill. I saw the Glory of God on you as soon as you walked through that door, John 6:27 talks about the seal of God."

"Mr. King what do I do now? I can't go back to that life and do what I used to do. I mean God took the taste of cigarettes, drugs and alcohol from me. I have no desire for those things." "Daughter there is always a way out, but you have souls attached to you and God will be with you as he was with Moses. You can escape right now and never return to that place of bondage or you can go back and bring others out. It's up to you daughter God has his hands on you and no harm will come to you."

THE ASSIGNMENT

Zoya returned home and Ollie greeted her at the door. "Hey Babe, how was your date?" It grieved Zoya that he was calling her babe, but she had to be careful not to show it. Zoya tried to walk past Ollie and he grabbed her by the arm, and looked in her face. "You look very different, like I don't even know who you are? What kind of event did you attend tonight Zoya?" "I attended a church event." Ollie laughed, "Get the hell out of here. A Pastor wanted to get his freak on at a church event?" Ollie laughed and said, "Well that is my kind of guy, no judgement zone over here Babe." "No Ollie, that is not what happened. He prayed for me and with me." Zoya looked from the floor in to Ollie's eyes, and he noticed that God was with her. Ollie was speechless for the first time and Zoya said, "Goodnight." Ollie watched her go upstairs and it looked as if she was floating. Ollie looked at the brown liquor in his glass and said, "I think I had too much to drink tonight."

As the following days went by, Zoya started to pray more and Ollie was becoming frustrated with her. He would send her out on more dates, and Zoya would minister to the men who were about to cheat on their wives. The Lord was with her even when men would get drunk. God would have them not touch her. Zoya was being requested more as a counselor than a hooker. Ollie didn't like it one bit. A basketball player requested a call girl for the weekend and Ollie knew that he was a bad boy. He thought this man was just what Zoya needed. When Zoya arrived at Miami airport she was picked up in a limo with instructions to get ready for a wild weekend. There were bottles of Champaign, cocaine and weed for her enjoyment. The old Zoya would have indulged, but this new heart was not interested.

Once Zoya arrived at this mansion she prayed, "Lord is this my assignment?" The famous basketball player (Jamie) was out, and left instructions for her to dress for a pool party that he was throwing that night. Later that night Zoya looked out of her window and saw that the DJ was setting up and all the women were hanging out by the pool with drinks in their hands. Zoya was nervous, and she used to drink to calm down her nerves. She prayed, and she dressed in her bathing suit to enter the party. As she entered the party, all eyes were on her and people wanted to know who she was. There was a glow on her that no one had ever seen before. Jamie stopped groping women and he couldn't take his eyes off Zoya. He walked over to her and said, "You must be Zoya," and he kissed her cheek in lust. Zoya shook his hand, prayed inwardly and the power of God was on her. Immediately, Jamie removed his hand from her not knowing what he was feeling at the moment, but his buzz left him. Therefore, he went to get another drink to shake off what he was feeling. Zoya met a few women at the pool and was having a great conversation.

A few hours went by and a wild and confused Jamie appeared cursing people out telling them to get out of his house. No one understood what was going on, so they began to leave. Zoya went into the house and retreated to her room not knowing what was going on. Jamie entered her room, and asked her in an unprofessional way to get out of his house. Zoya asked if he was ok, and she followed behind pleading with him to tell her what was going on. Jamie finally broke down and said that his mother was in a car accident and they told him that she might not make it. Jamie fell to his knees crying and Zoya began to pray. First, she prayed in a low voice, and then she began to pray a little louder. Zoya's request was a miracle from God for Jamie's mom. Jamie felt the presence of God while Zoya prayed, and he prayed with her. They prayed for an hour, and Jamie thanked her for supporting him. Jamie was flying home to see his mother, and Zoya returned to New York. Ollie was getting more and more annoyed with Zoya because she was affecting his business and his other daughters. It was time to teach the holy whore a lesson. When Zoya returned home, Spice was in her room waiting for her. Zoya understood that Spice did not like her, but she had to show Godly love. Then out of the blue, Spice attacked Zoya by hitting her on the side of her face with a hammer. She kept kicking Zoya saying, "You tried to take my place, but I'm the Queen of this castle. Your protection is over. Ollie said I could do anything I want to you, and I'm going to enjoy killing you."

Zoya could remember a sermon that her grandfather taught years ago, when Jesus was on the cross and his last words were, "Father forgive them for they know not what they do," and she blacked out.

As Zoya began to open her eyes, she realized that she was in a hospital with so many flowers. A nurse was standing over her saying, "Welcome back to the land of the living, Zoya." Zoya tried to speak, but couldn't, and then he walked through the doors... Dr. Grinn. Dr. Grinn pulled the tube from her throat and said, "We must stop meeting like this young lady." Zoya smiled and said, "What happened to me?" Dr. Grinn said "You were attacked and assaulted by a woman with a hammer. You were in a coma four months Zoya, but you've had quite a few visitors and prayer warriors by your bedside. Jamie Rolland paid for your hospital bills and wanted you to know that his mother is doing well. Jamie said that you have a friend for life, and that you prayed for his mother's healing and God did it! He claims to be a born-again Christian." Zoya was so happy that tears were in her eyes of pure happiness. "A few women came by to see you with very unusual names and have been camping out at this hospital. A very special Pastor assured me that you were going to be fine. He explained to me that God had you all along through your journey."

After a few weeks in the hospital, Zoya recovered and was released. Zoya got to know Dr. Grinn a little better and realized that the crush she had on him was still there. Dr. Grinn never married because he told Zoya he was waiting for her to grow up. Dr. Grinn asked Zoya to be his wife because he loved her from the first moment he laid eyes on her. He knew in his heart that one day she would be his wife. Dr. Grinn smiled and said, "Pastor King told me to marry you before someone else did." Two years later they were married. Zoya won so many souls to the Kingdom of God by being in an uncomfortable place so that his Glory could show up. It was reported in the news that Ollie and Spice were burned in a fire. Apparently, Ollie in his drunken stupor fell asleep with a cigarette in his hand which burned down his house and took their lives. After two years, it was time for Zoya to go home and see Nana.

Zoya pulled up to the house that she ran away from as a teenager. As she stepped onto the porch to ring the doorbell, Nana was coming out of her house. "May I help you dear?" Nana said. Nana looked different. She aged, but she still had the fire in her eyes. I said, "Nana it's me." Nana looked at me and said, "Me who?" I laughed and said, "Zoya, Nana." Nana touched my face and said, "Zoya is that really you?" I smiled with tears in my eyes. I couldn't believe that I had already forgiven Nana years ago, and to see her only confirmed that love conquers all ailments in the heart. I felt free to love these women with all my heart. I hugged Nana, and we cried together. I asked Nana to forgive me, and to my surprise she asked me for forgiveness. I felt the power of God around us.

Nana invited me in the house and made me some tea. We talked for what seemed like hours. Nana said she prayed every day for me, and God dealt with her. I shared my experience with Nana, and what I did while I was in New York. I also shared that I married Dr. Grinn and Nana laughed. I asked Nana, "Why are you laughing?" Nana said that the Lord showed her a long time ago that I was going to leave her for Dr. Grinn and that's why she didn't like him. We laughed together. I told Nana that I had a small church in Brooklyn, NY where I pastored troubled youth and young women. I said, "I remember when Grandpa Joe died. He visited me while I was resting in the chapel to tell me that I would minister to a lot of women during my journey. Nana I am proud to say that our church is an intervention for women to avoid prostitution. If it wasn't for the path I took, I would have never been able to rescue these beautiful young women. The battle of the calling was greater than the calling of the streets, Nana. Now I'm finally happy in the Lord, married to a wonderful doctor, and I am pregnant with your grandchild." Nana was in tears and I said, "It's going to be a boy, and I will name him Zion after my father."

Zoya put Nana's hand over her belly and said, "It's time for healing and new beginnings in our family." 2 Chronicles 7:14, "If my people who are called by my name would humble themselves and pray, seek my face; and turn from their wicked ways, then I will hear from heaven and forgive their sin and will heal their land.

ABOUT THE AUTHOR

Trevolia Marie Booker Pershay, known as Trevi to her friends and colleagues, grew up in Brooklyn, East New York Projects (Louise H. Pink Houses), where she was reared by a strong, single, black woman. Trevi was molested by a woman when she was 8 years old, and then again by a male when she was 9 years old. These scars left Trevi trying to rediscover who she was. After joining the Nation of Islam, who were known as the five percenters at that time. Trevi thought that understanding who we were as African Americans would give her guidance in who she was as a Queen in this universe. However, she realized that it was just a way to seduce young women into having babies, and Trevi wanted more.

Trevi used dance as an avenue of healing to escape from her sadness and pain. What she didn't understand was that there were other women out there like herself. At 16, Trevi started a dance organization in her community center that attracted over 35 girls in the program. Trevi knew that she was on to something and years later, PDM Performing Arts Corporation was birthed. Trevi came back to the community of Brooklyn and implemented programs that would change the lives of some many young people.

As CEO and founder for PDM Performing Arts Corporation and Trevi Pershay Productions, her goal is inspiring others to know that life is a gift from God and it's up to us to utilize it wisely. The dance program reached over 300 youth in the past 18 years, and the plays have inspired people of all ages in the community.

Thus far, Trevi has written 15 plays, and working on a web-series and a sitcom. When she was depressed and tried to take her life, God gave her so many chances to live because He knew that purpose was knocking, and Destiny was on the other side of that door. Trevi says, "The world better get ready for me because I'm coming for everything people said I couldn't have."

Made in the USA
Middletown, DE
09 July 2022